LIGHTNING
BOLT
BOOKS™

The Supersmart Parrot

Mari Schuh

Lerner Publications ◆ Minneapolis

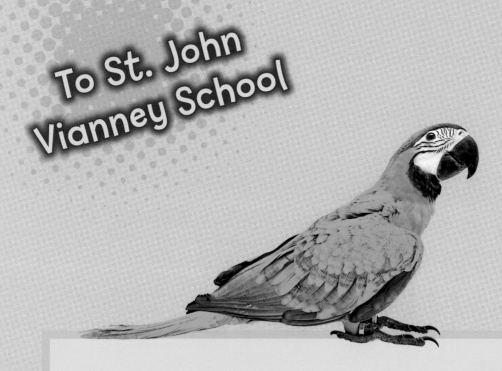

To St. John Vianney School

Lerner Publications Company
A division of Lerner Publishing Group, Inc.
241 First Avenue North
Minneapolis, MN 55401 USA

For reading levels and more information, look up this title at www.lernerbooks.com.

Library of Congress Cataloging-in-Publication Data

Names: Schuh, Mari C., 1975- author.
Title: The supersmart parrot / Mari Schuh.
Description: Minneapolis : Lerner Publications, [2018] | Series: Lightning bolt books. Supersmart animals | Audience: Ages 6–9. | Audience: K to grade 3. | Includes bibliographical references and index.
Identifiers: LCCN 2017044486 (print) | LCCN 2017054024 (ebook) | ISBN 9781541525344 (eb pdf) | ISBN 9781541519824 (lb : alk. paper) | ISBN 9781541527652 (pb : alk. paper)
Subjects: LCSH: Parrots—Behavior—Juvenile literature. | Parrots—Psychology—Juvenile literature.
Classification: LCC QL696.P7 (print) | LCC QL696.P7 S38 2018 (ebook) | DDC 598.7/1—dc23

LC record available at https://lccn.loc.gov/2017044486

Manufactured in the United States of America
1-44318-34564-3/22/2018

Table of Contents

Meet the Parrot

Two parrots squawk in the rain forest. They screech and chirp. These supersmart birds make loud noises to communicate with each other.

Parrots often live in large groups called flocks.

Parrots usually live in warm areas. But some parrots live on mountains and in snowy forests.

There are more than 360 kinds of parrots. They all have curved beaks and strong toes with sharp claws.

Parrots called macaws have bright red, yellow, and blue feathers.

Smart Parrots

Some parrots use tools to eat. Sticks help them break open nuts. Sometimes parrots use leaves to hold food in place so they can eat with their strong beaks.

Eating shells helps parrots make strong eggs.

Parrots also use rocks to break seashells into small pieces. Then the parrots eat the shell pieces.

Male cockatoo parrots even use tools to make music. They bang sticks, rocks, or shells on tree branches to attract mates. The branch works like a drum.

This is an African gray parrot.

Some African gray parrots in the wild can mimic the sounds of birds and bats. Parrots that live with people also mimic sounds and words they hear.

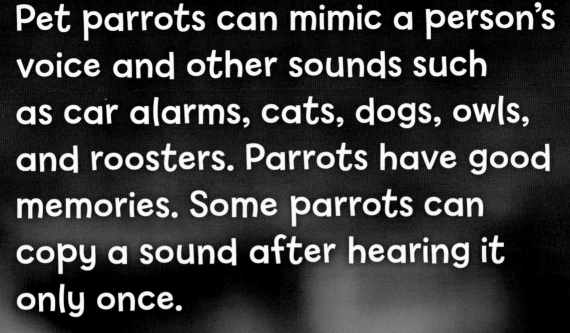

Pet parrots can mimic a person's voice and other sounds such as car alarms, cats, dogs, owls, and roosters. Parrots have good memories. Some parrots can copy a sound after hearing it only once.

Parrots may ask for their favorite treats by name.

The Life of a Parrot

Female parrots lay two to eight eggs at a time. Males and females often take turns sitting on the eggs to keep them warm.

Chicks usually hatch from their eggs in about a month. The tiny chicks have no feathers. They start to grow feathers in a few weeks. Both parents feed the tiny chicks.

Parrots eat fruit, nuts, seeds, and insects.

Parrots grow to be many different sizes. Some tiny parrots are only about 3 inches (8 cm) tall. Other parrots grow to be 40 inches (102 cm).

The hyacinth macaw is the largest kind of parrot.

These colorful birds live for about thirty to fifty years. But some parrots live for eighty years.

Parrots in Danger

Some kinds of parrots are in danger of going extinct. Hawks, eagles, and jaguars try to eat parrots.

Sometimes people destroy parrot habitats to build farms and roads. Then parrots have fewer places to live. People also take parrots from the wild to sell as pets.

Cutting down trees destroys a parrot's habitat.

But some people are working
hard to keep parrots safe.
They keep trees from being
cut down. They make safe
areas where parrots can live
and make nests.

Laws stop some parrots from being sold as pets. These laws help keep parrots in their habitat. Many people around the world are working hard to protect these supersmart birds.

Parrot Diagram

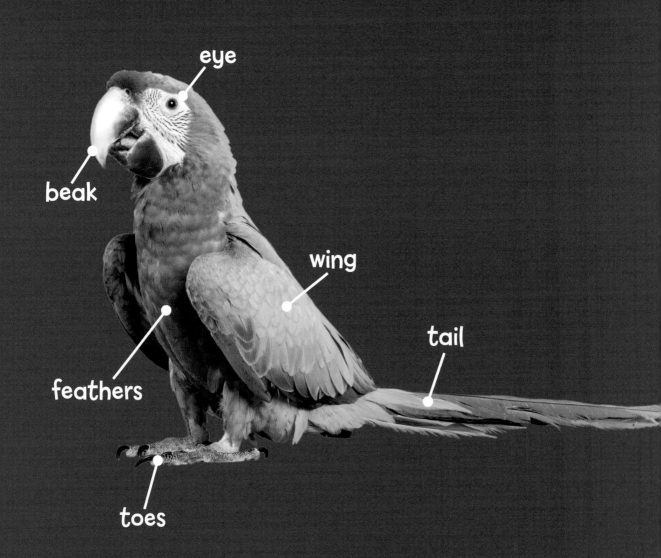

eye

beak

wing

tail

feathers

toes

Fun Facts

- Parrots use their strong feet to grip tools and food. They usually prefer to use one foot more than the other foot, just as humans are left- or right-handed.

- Some African grey parrots have learned to count. They also know shapes, colors, and more than seven hundred words.

- Some parrots can learn to open special locks. They have to do many things to get the locks to open. These parrots can take out pins and screws and move bolts to open the locks.

Glossary

communicate: to pass along information

extinct: having died out

habitat: the place where an animal lives

hatch: to come out of an egg

jaguar: a large wildcat

mate: a partner

mimic: to copy what another animal or a person sounds like

rain forest: a thick area of trees where a lot of rain falls

Further Reading

Bozzo, Linda. *When Parrots Speak.* New York: Enslow, 2017.

Donohue, Moira Rose. *Parrot Genius! And More True Stories of Amazing Animal Talents.* Washington, DC: National Geographic, 2014.

Easy Science for Kids: Parrots—Over 350 Types
http://easyscienceforkids.com/all-about-parrots

Enchanted Learning: African Gray Parrot
http://www.enchantedlearning.com/subjects
/birds/printouts/Grayparrotprintout.shtml

San Diego Zoo Kids: Hyacinth Macaw
http://kidssandiegozoo.org/videos/hyacinth
-macaw

Sill, Cathryn. *About Parrots: A Guide for Children.* Atlanta: Peachtree, 2014.

Index

Photo Acknowledgments

The images in this book are used with the permission of: SmileKorn/Shutterstock.com, p. 2; Scoobydoo2/iStock/Getty Images, p. 4; Nonthawatst/Shutterstock.com, p. 5; Maciej Czekajewski/Shutterstock.com, p. 6; Pareena/Shutterstock.com, p. 7; Valery Evlakhov/Shutterstock.com, p. 8; egilshay/Shutterstock.com, p. 9; viper345/Shutterstock.com, p. 10; kunmom/Shutterstock.com, p. 11; YK/Shutterstock.com, pp. 12, 13; Bildagentur Zoonar GmbH/Shutterstock.com, p. 14; Ondrej Prosicky/Shutterstock.com, pp. 15, 18; Jamen Percy/Shutterstock.com, p. 16; Lisette van der Kroon/Shutterstock.com, p. 17; sompreaw/Shutterstock.com, p. 19; LifetimeStock/Shutterstock.com, p. 20; Butterfly Hunter/Shutterstock.com, p. 22.

Front cover: cbenjasuwan/iStock/Getty Images.

Main body text set in Billy Infant regular 28/36. Typeface provided by SparkType.